A Garland Series

The English Stage
Attack and Defense 1577 - 1730

A collection of 90 important works
reprinted in photo-facsimile in 50 volumes

edited by
Arthur Freeman
Boston University

The Danger of Masquerades and Raree-Shows

C. R.

The Dancing Devils

Or, the Roaring Dragon

Anonymous

A Letter to My Lord*******

on the Present Diversions of the Town

Anonymous

with a preface
for the Garland Edition by

Arthur Freeman

Garland Publishing, Inc., New York & London

1974

Library of Congress Cataloging in Publication Data
Main entry under title:

The Danger of masquerades and raree-shows.

Reprint of 3 works: the 1st, printed for W. Boreham,
London, 1718; the 2d, by E. Ward, printed and sold by
A. Bettesworth, London, 1724; and the 3d, printed for
J. Roberts, London, 1725, respectively.
        1. Performing arts--England--History--Sources.
I. C. R. II. R., C. III. Ward, Edward, 1667-1731.
The dancing devils. 1974. IV. Title: The dancing
devils. V. A Letter to my Lord*******on the present
diversions of the town. 1974.
PN2593.D3 1974   790.2'0942   76-170488
ISBN 0-8240-0629-1

Printed in the United States of America

Preface

Not only the expectable antagonism of church and state threatened, by fits and starts, the livelihood of the English stage in its latter years of franchised establishment, but ironically, from within came what Allardyce Nicoll terms "rival entertainment," to test the popularity of the legitimate theater as its dramatists and actors had by now defined it. Pantomimes, masquerades, "raree-shows" (narrated peepshows), music at Vauxhall, bestial, monstrous, and freakish human exhibitions, hearkening back to the bullring, fencing-house, and bear garden of Elizabethan professional entertainment, competed for the attention of early-eighteenth-century pleasure-seekers. And in fact the pantomimists could boast an almost total victory over traditional farce by c. 1725 (cf. Leo Hughes, A Century of English Farce *[Princeton, 1956], pp. 118 ff.; Hughes also discusses "raree-shows," pp. 94-129* passim*), although the dynamic success of* The Beggar's Opera *and its imitations about leveled the temporary imbalance. Yet well past mid-century farce and pantomime continued neck-and-neck with nearly equal popularity in London attendance. We have little concrete evidence of the nature of early theatrical pantomime, and perhaps the best descriptions are offered by the extant parodies of this silent* genre *(see*

5

PREFACE

Nicoll, History of English Drama, 1660-1900, *II, 251-8, and Leo Hughes, as above).* The Dancing Devils *(1724), like several of its kind but probably the most amusing, presents a sham-pantomime nominally parodic of the hateful and "rival" dumbshow. We reprint the Yale copy (Beinecke Ik w211 724), collating A-H⁴I³. Lowe-Arnott-Robinson 865.*

Virtually all of C. R.'s indignant, if satiric, pamphlet is epitomized on its title page, and the dedication to Anne Oldfield, one of the most distinguished of professional actresses, speaks for the bias of the writer. Our reprint is from a copy in the British Museum (11794.d.38), collating π¹B⁴B-D⁴E². Lowe-Arnott-Robinson 864. A Letter to My Lord *******, *which fixes much of its blame upon the three principal stage-managers, also courses the threat of eccentric or alternative entertainment, opera and masquerades, against which the beset theater struggled in the years between Betterton and Garrick, with few but irrepressible John Gay, perhaps, for a creative champion in the dangerous 1720s and '30s. And herein may lie one explanation of the crisis: what truly exciting new drama, save Gay's, and at a remove George Lillo's, do we associate with those decades of Swift, Pope, Defoe, Addison and Steele? We reprint* A Letter *(Lowe-Arnott-Robinson 866) from the British Museum copy (641.e.17[14]), collating A²B-D⁴E¹; the half title, missing in the BM copy, has been supplied from a copy at Harvard.*

May, 1973   A.F.

THE
DANGER
OF
Masquerades and Raree-shows,
OR THE
Complaints of the Stage,
AGAINST

Masquerades, Opera's, Assemblies, Balls, Puppet-shows, Bear-gardens, Cock-fights, Wrestling, Posture-masters, Cudgel-playing, Foot-ball, Rope-dancing, Merry-makings, and several other irrational Entertainments, as being the Ground and Occasion of the late Decay of Wit in the Island of *Great-Britain.*

By *C. R.* of *C. C. C. Oxford.*

Inscribed to Mrs. OLDFIELD.

LONDON,
Printed for W. BOREHAM, at the *Angel* in *Pater-noster-Row,* 1718.

(Price Six-pence.)

TO
Mrs. OLDFIELD.

MADAM,

'TIS not only the Apprehension of the *Vulgar*, (who are every Day remarkable for their Stupid Conjectures) but also *Persons* of no small Penetration have been alarm'd at the great Number of *Raree-Shows*, which of late have pass'd under our Windows. And some who had a high Idea of the *King* of *Sicily*'s Politicks, cou'd not be perswaded but that the *Puppets* might start up into *Armies*, while the Master of the *Engine* was a *General* in disguise ready to head the Inchanted *Enemy*. But *Heaven* which has always protected this *Nation* both

B

against

DEDICATION.

against publick and private Assaults, inspired some of our Zealous *Magistrates*, happily to surprise these invisible Camps before they cou'd bring about their suspected Designs. — I own, I am not quite so extravagant in my Speculations; yet I cannot but think the sudden Appearance of these *Savoyards*; did prognosticate some dangerous *Revolution*; not of the *Government*, (which *Puppets* cannot expect to Subvert, when whole Armies of more than Men, have been so often repuls'd) but of some other Branch of our Happiness. And according to my Divination, they seem to have been a *Providential* Warning of that overgrown *Raree-Show:* The *Masquerade*, which was lately exhibited to the great Detriement of Wit, and Ingenuity. However, I will stand Corrected in my Opinion, by those

who

DEDICATION.

who can give a better Account of the
Surprife the *Town* has been in upon
that Occafion. Now, *Madam*, the
Stage (where you have long Reign'd
Abfolute) being the chief *Staple* of
Wit, I make bold to remind you of
the Danger your *Charge* is in, unlefs
the *Publick* be well Guarded againft
the Attack: The *Mob* will always be
Incorrigible upon this Head, but
fuch as are capable to diftinguifh between Mrs. *Oldfield* npon the Stage,
and the *Muffl'd Crew* in the *Hay-market*:
will never forgive themfelves that
Piece of Prodigality, in paying three
Guineas and a Half to fee Nature in
a *Mafque*, inftead of a Crown to fee
her in her own *Shape*. They only
give a *Dark Leffon* which none under-
ftand but fuch as are Accuftom'd to
difcourfe by Signs; whereas you give
a fine turn to good Senfe and Breeding,

DEDICATION.

ing, by a quick and prevailing Method. You entertain our *Reason*, they amuse the *Sense* with a Suspension of *Reason*. You enter into the *Passions*, and *Follies* of Mankind, and discover the *Fort*, and the *Foible* of all Stations. They Administer Matter for your *Ridicule*, or *Compassion*. You in fine live a Rational Life, they an Animal Life. And that the *Stage* may always Flourish, (as it never can fail while it is under the Influence of so powerful a *Protectrix*) is the constant wish of one, who is no farther a Friend to *Masquerades* than by being unwilling to discover how much he is.

MADAM,

Your great Admirer

and most humble

Servant. *C. R.*

THE
PREFACE.

AS I return'd the other Day from visiting a Friend in the City, two Things very much surpriz'd me. One was the Idle Posture of the Goldsmiths in Lombard-street, the other was the Melancholy Aspect of the Booksellers in St. Paul's-Church-yard. The first was owing to the Scarcity of Silver, the latter to a Decay of Wit. And as a Distemper naturally calls out for a Cure, so within my self I assum'd the Quality of a Physician. I overlook'd the first Misfortune as too big for my Care, and besides being a Politick Evil, it seem'd to require a National Consultation to draw Men out of the Surprise. The other appear'd to be any Mans Business, wherefore using the common Freedom of other Sons of Adam, I was resolved to probe the bottom of the Wound, and make an Essay towards restoring those Smuglers of Learning the Booksellers, to a Pristine Serenity of Countenance.

That

The PREFACE.

That a bright Nation *shou'd become* Dull, *and* Insipid, *is somewhat suitable to other Steps of* Divine Providence, *which is remarkable for Variety in that Kind.* And *if all* Sublunary *things are subject to change, why may we not expect to see an Ebbing, and Flowing of* Wit ? Nature *puts a stop to the Growth of all other Productions, and feeds them only that they may Subsist, not that they may increase to a* Gigantick Size. The keenest Appetite *may be Cloy'd.* And *every* Nation *has a non-plus ultra in the way of Trade.* And *why may not there be a glut as well of Wit, as of Merchandize, or Victuals?* A few Years ago, Dunkirk *was a rich, and flourishing Town; now 'tis a Nest of Beggars.* And *why?* Their Stock *is Spent, and they have no Import.* In a Word, *if the brightest* Beauties *are obliged to submit to an Alteration, and the Sun it self sometimes suffers a Total* Ecclipse, *the British* Nation *must not pretend to be exempt from the common Fate.*

THE

THE
DANGER
OF
MASQUERADES and RAREE-SHOWS,
OR THE
Complaints of the STAGE, &c.

Have for a confiderable time
been a private *Obferver* of what
I now prefume to make publick: And it was a very irk-
fome Meditation in my retir'd
Moments, to reflect that *Show* Shou'd be prefer'd to *intrinfick* Merit; the *Fidler*, to the

Philosopher, and a *Knave* under a *Masque* to those who never refus'd to appear barefac'd in the most *Critical* Seasons. This degenerate State of the *Nation* in regard of *Wit* moved me with a compassionate Curiosity, to look into the grounds, and occasion of it. And upon a general Survey of the abuse, I found it proceeded from attributing too much to the *Senses*, and too little to the *Judgment*. Men of *Wit*, who Studied to refine the Soul were discountenanc'd, and only those caress'd who cou'd give the Senses an Animal Amusement. Now as no Distemper comes to a head on a suddain, so this grand Enemy to *Liberal Sciences* call'd a *Masquerade* was usher'd into the Nation by little irrational Entertainments, wich all look'd the same way, and took their rise from the Populace, Stupidity, and want of Reflexion. For as *Nits* by assembling together in corners do grow into Lice, so *Puppet-Shows*, *Raree-Shows*, *Balls*, *Assemblies*, and *Opera's* by a quick growth became a *Masquerade*. But that the Cure of this dangerous Distemper may be render'd Compleat, I will look into the Origin of this woeful Revolt from *Wit*, to *Stupidity*.

Lesser

Leſſer Failings in point of *Wit* have been a long time bore with, as chiefly reigning among *Perſons* of no Conſequence. ———— And tho' now and then a *Man of Diſtinction*, was ſeen at the *Bear-garden*, or ſhowing his Parts in *Lincolns-Inn-fields*, 'tis only of late that a *General Defection* has been obſerv'd, and that the Wit of the *Stage* has been obliged to give way to the *dumb Pageantry* of a *Maſquerade*. When firſt I heard a deſcription of one of thoſe *noble Exhibitions*, it ſeem'd to me that either the *Nation* had committed ſome notorious Villany, or that they were prepar'd to do it, becauſe they durſt not ſhow their Face. And indeed, they have committed the greateſt of *Villanies* ; Wit is aſſaſſinated, and in a *Maſque* too, that the *Murtherer* may better eſcape the hand of juſtice.

But to enter upon the Cauſe. This *Rare-Show* where *H——r* turns the Key to ſet the *Puppets* a dancing has no other claim to Ingenuity than what is derived from a *Learned Taylor*, or a *Nimble Butler*; All the intrinſick worth conſiſts in the Beauties of the Back and Belly. Oh! what a glorious Entertainment will be for *Poſterity* half a *Century* hence, to

B   call

call over the famous Atchievements of their Ancestors, who in such a *Kings* Reign, in such a year of our *Lord*, and on such a day of the *Month*, were so Ingenious as to put a *Taylor* in mind of shaping a Piece of Velvet into a *Spanish Doublet* to the great Admiration of all Spectators? And what a remarkable *Epocha* of domestick Occurrences will it be to date them from the time that noble Trophy was hung up in the Wardrobe, with the Learned Observation of. *This was my Grandsires Dress at such a Masquerade?*

Wit has been visibly upon the Decay ever since the Nation seem'd inclin'd to prefer *Haymarket* to *Drury-lane:* And the Pleasures of Sense, to the Beauties of the Mind. *Musick* at the most is but *Noise* under different Modifications, and Effects the *Ear*, as Colours affect the *Eye:* But neither reach the Soul. Both *Seeing*, and *Hearing* are irrational, and Animal Entertainments. Some make it a great Question whether a *Poet* ought to be esteem'd a *Wit*; because the Singularity of the Performance which shou'd purchase him that Name is all *Musical*. The best *Poems* are only common Sense, with the advantage of of *Jingle* and *Rhime*; which diverts the Ear but improves not the Understanding. Those celebrated Verses of Mr. *Dryden* upon the Duke of *Buckingham*.

Who in the Space of one Revolving Moon,
was Fidler, Statesman, Chymist, and Buffoon.

Only amount to this piece of poor, vulgar, common Sense, *vid.* His *Grace the Duke of Buckingham was seldom of the same mind a Month together.* So that the Perfection of *Poetry* is to put a good Tune to prose, and the *Poet* and the *Fidler* are almost equal in their claim as to *Wit*. Rubbing a few *Horse-hairs* upon *Cat-guits*, or rising higher, or lower with a Mans Voice are but poor *Topicks*, to render a Nation famous. Ay, but Musick is Divine, and full of Charms. I allow some People's Fingers are more manageable than others. And one has a more open Throat, a clearer Pipe, Teeth better adapted to articulate sound than another; but at the same time, this is all a Mechanical Advantage, still there is no Inconsistence between a *Fool*, and a *Musician*.

Assemblies are no less of ill Consequence than *Masquerades*. *Avarice*, and *Lust*, are

the

the two Capital Inducements to meet upon
such Occasions. But neither of them require
much Wit. There may be *Craft* indeed, in
shaking the Elbow, and dealing out the
Cards, as also something of Management in
carrying on an *Amorous Intrigue*; but a
Blockhead is as capable to nick the Main, as a
Man of Sense; and there is no occasion to be
a *Philosopher* for a Man to cuckhold his
Neighbour. A good Assurance, and a Purse
of Gold will do the *Feat*.

Balls are still a greater Prejudice to *Wit*.
They pluck it up by the very Roots, by de-
stroying *Thought*, and *Reflection*, and expo-
sing *Mortals* to a continual Dissipation of
Mind. 'Tis indeed an *Ingenious Enquiry*;
to find out who and who were Partners at a
Country Dance. And turning sometimes to
the Right, and sometimes to the Left, may
be of great Importance to human Kind. And
'tis about as much a Subject of Triumph to
cut a *Capre* three quarters of a yard high, as
to step upon one of the Benches in the *Mall*;
and so leap down again. I know no Sub-
stantial Difference there is between shuffling
a Mans Feet upon the Ground, and playing

with

with his Cravat. Is not Mr. *Clinch* preferable
to *Nicholini* in variety of Noise-Wit? It wou'd
be too low and trivial an Obfervation, to infift
much upon the *Antipathy* there is between
Wit, and thofe vulgar Paftimes, *Rope-dancing*, *Foot-ball*, *Wreftling*, *Puppet-fhows*, &c.
Yet it will not be amifs to mention them
upon that Account. For tho' broken Shins,
broken Heads, Contufions, Diflocations, unmannerly Grinning, Hoarfnefs, and offenfive
Vociferations, are only the immediate Effect
of thofe Paftimes, yet they difcover the
Want, and very much incline Mankind to a
Decay of Wit.

But that I may yet make a farther Difco-
very of the Nature of this Diftemper, I will
reduce the occafions of the decay of *Wit*, to
thefe three Heads. Some may be efteem'd
Natural; others *Moral*; others *Politick*.
Some are not witty, becaufe 'tis not in their
Power, *others* are too good *Chriftians* to be
witty; a *Third* fort are deterr'd from it by a
Principle of *Self-Prefervation*. 'Tis a Con-
troverted Point, whether there be any difference in the natural Perfections of the Soul.
This is a Piece of Curiofity I am not willing

to

to dwell upon; tho' indeed it appears to me, as if the only Difference were in the *Organization* of the Body. A *Wit* becomes a *Madman* by having something displac'd in his Head; and a *Natural Fool* would have been a *wise Man*, if some Accident had not disturb'd the Formation of the *Fœtus*. A *Fool* is crippl'd in his Brain, as one that has a short Leg is crippl'd in that Member. Yet we cannot say there is any Defect in the *Soul*, in either Case. But to wave this Point, among the *Natural Impediments* of Wit, the *Climate* may be consider'd in the first Place. The *Sun* certainly has a strong Influence upon the lower World; it affects not only the *Earth*, and the *Air*, but also *Human Bodies*; and by Concomitancy gives some kind of turn to the Passions of the Soul. In the *Indies*, it produces *Silver*, *Gold*, and *Diamonds*. In the Southern Parts of *Europe*, *Wine*, *Marble*, *Oranges*, *Olives*, &c. Towards the North it is prolific in *Rocks*, *Heath*, *Crabbs*, *Gooseberries*, *Hops*, *Beer*, *Potatoes*. And why this Difference in the Fruits of the Earth? But because the Rays of the *Sun* are more Feeble, the nearer she approacheth to the Northern

Pole:

Pole: So that many of her Productions in such *Latitudes* may be look'd upon as the *Abortives of Natures.* *Human Bodies* in like manner lie under the same Influence: It is attributed to the stranger, or weaker Vibrations of the Sun, that some of the Inhabitants of the *Earth* are *black*, others *tawny*, others *white*. By the same Method, Man's Size is alter'd, as well as his Colour. The *Southern Women* cease to bear Children soon after Twenty; the stubborn *Northern Lass* holds out till near Fifty. All which proceeds very much from the Difference of Climates. Yes, both Sickness and Health, depend in many Respects upon the Power of the Sun. A dull, hazy Day, disturbs the Temperament of the *Body*, and setts the Humours afloat, whereas a bright Season draws them out and dissolves 'em in the Air, by way of Perspiration. *Mediterranean Countreys* are not so subject to dull Influences as Islands. There the *Air* is thin, and refin'd, here thick, and moist. This occasioneth a difference in the Passions, and penetration of the *Inhabitants*. Under this Head we may consider *Diet* was very much conducing to

render

render Persons dull, or sprightly. *Beef*, *Mutton*, *Pudding*, and generally all Butchers Meat, (unless the animal Parts be very much sublimated by a skillful Hand) are a great Enemy to Wit; But *Chicks*, *Quails*, *Teals*, *Beccaficas*, &c. are the proper Food for *Ingenuity*. What made D----y, T----e, and several others such stupid Writers, but frequenting Chop-houses? whereas, half a Guinea now, and then, laid out at *Brawns*, or *Pontacks*, wou'd have turn'd to Advantage, by the effect it wou'd have had upon their *Intellectuals*. Living too long in a small *Edifice* call'd a *Box*, confines the Ideas; a Coal fire spoils the Furniture of the Mind. To drink Beer instead of Wine, lowers *Wit* so much *per Cent*; and in a few Years it will change a Person of the most refin'd *Genius* into a mere *Rapsodist*.

Another Occasion of the *Decay* of Wit is, the great Mistake some *Pretenders* that Way lye under, as to the Call of *Nature*. No Man is bless'd with an universal *Genius*. How many excellent *Plow-men* are daily spoil'd by putting on a *Parsons Gown*. And how many Factious *Statesmen* injure the Publick

lick by miftaking the *Court* for a *Coffee-House*. What an awkward Sight is it to fee a *Dancing-Mafter* lead up an *Army*, or the *Captain* of a Man of War riding a Race at *New-market*. The want of attending to this Call of Nature, fills the World with Nonfenfe, Mifmanagement, and Improper, ties in every Station of Life.

Again ; The Nation at prefent feems as much miftaken in the *Idea* of *Wit*, as they are in their *Call* to that Employment. Some take a *Wit* and a *wife Man* to be the fame Thing. Indeed in *Old Times*, every Virtuous Man was efteem'd a *Wit* ; becaufe his Sentiments diftinguifh'd him from the Common of Mankind, and he made himfelf admir'd for a laudable Singularity in his Conduct. Others in the other extreme, take a *Wit* to be a Man of barren Speculations, who glories in neglecting what is of real ufe to Mankind. A third Sort wou'd be efteem'd Wits upon account of correcting *Solecifms*, and falfe *Punctuations*, and digging for *Etymologies*. And the Generality of Men are willing to confound Me*mory*, with *Wit*, as if Wit confifted in carrying Burdens, and Loading the

Memory

Memory with Words. Nor is the Number
of those less who regard Wit as an absolute
Quality, which some may be Masters of in
all its Latitude. But the Truth is, 'tis all
respective, tied to *Places, Terms, Seasons,* and
different Employments. He that is a Wit in
one Respect, may expose himself in many
others. One that is *Wise* in the Drawing
Room, may be a *Fool* in the *Dairy.* A Coun-
try-Gentleman perhaps is as ignorant of the
Difference between a *Maid of Honour,* and a
Lady of the Bed-Chamber ; as a *Courtier* is
incapable to distinguish between a fat Sheep
and lean one, and a notable Blunder either
way, shews that every Man is a *Fool* in what
he does not understand. I was once acquainted with a very Learned Foreign Divine,
who notwithstanding was puzzled with the
Query ; whether Travellers went by Land
or Sea, from *Callis* to *Dover.* The Scripture
will make an excellent Divine, but it does
not give a Map either of *France* or *Eng-
land.*

In the next place, I am to consider the
Moral Impediments of *Wit.* In a leud Age,
a *Moral Wit* is very little relish'd. *Rochester*

is

is almost every Bodies Book. *Cowley* is more admir'd than *Read*. What a World do we live in, that a Man must abjure *Christianity* to become *Witty!* Purge the *Book-sellers* Shops of *Satyr*, and *Smut*, and there is nothing to give a moral Man an Hours Diversion. A *Play* is what most Persons have recourse to for a little Relaxations ; And what is it we laugh at upon that occasion? Either to see a Man stumble over a Block, or to hear that he is Cuckolded. That is ; we never seem'd pleas'd, but either with *Impertinence*, or *Impiety*. A serious moral Scene, is every Bodies Aversion. As for what requires Study, it can have no Diversion in it, and less Ingenuity. What Wit is there in an *Act of Parliament*, *Bishop Hoadleys Controversies*, or Sir *Isaac Newtons* Demonstrations? They neither divert nor improve, unless a Man turns *Recluse*, and locks himself up four Days in a Week to understand their meaning. That *Engine* was certainly a *Master-piece* in its Kind, which mark'd out all the Moistions of the *Celestial Globe*, and Answer'd many intricate Questions belonging to *Astronomy* ; but if he that is tied up to Minutes, must Study two

C 2   Hours

Hours before he can learn what a Clock it is, there may be Wit in the *Invention*, but the *Treasure* lies too deep to be worth while to dig for it. But to return from this Digreſſion. Too much Religion, or a nicety in Morals, is certainly a very great Occaſion of the Scarcity of Wit. It does not only hinder Men of *bright Parts* from making their *Ideas* publick, but 'tis alſo a Reſtraint upon them in Converſation. I have known ſeveral *Conſcientious Wits* abſtain from *Jeſts, Puns,* and *Repartees,* partly for fear of taking a vanity in the *Performance*, and partly for fear of being tempted to a farther Impiety of becoming *extravagantly witty.* Perhaps it will be alledg'd againſt me, that my Arguments are inconſiſtent. For if Morality be one of the Grounds of the decay of Wit, how comes it that a *Nation* ſo extremely wicked, is ſo extremely dull ? To this it is eaſily reply'd ; That as the Sun ripens Fruit, ſo it is often the occaſion of its rotting and dropping from the Tree. And as a little Wine exhilerates the Soul and makes a Man *witty* ; ſo a little Liberty in Morals, gives Nature an Opportunity to ſhow her Vivacity : But when this
Liberty

Liberty is wretchedly improved into *Profane-ness*, it rifes above a Jeft, and does not divert the Ear, but makes it tingle. To laugh at a *Clergyman's* broad Hat is fometimes efteem'd a notable Piece of Wit, efpecially when 'tis roguifly perform'd. To mifapply a Text of *Scripture* to a ufe fomewhat profane, is a farther advance in the fame School. But to banter, and play with the number *Three* ; becaufe of the Reference it bears to the *Myftery* of the *Trinity* will fcarce pafs for Wit, unlefs it be in a Nation abandon'd to *Impiety*. So this Age has it in Election to embrace either Part of the Alternative. Either to renounce their Claim to *Wit*, or accept of it upon the Terms of *Impiety*.

The falfe *Idea* of *Wit*, which now *is* in vogue, excludes thofe from having any pretence to it, whofe Education otherwife wou'd back their Claim ; I mean the *Clergy*. For 'tis to be obferv'd, that *Learning* is not *Wit*, but often *Stupidity*. 'Tis not the *Movement-maker*, but the *Finifher* who challenges the Name of the celebrated *Watchmaker*. As Wit now goes, 'tis a rarity if not an impoffibility for a *Clergyman* to be witty without
breaking

breaking through his Character. Dr. S.——t
and some others are an Instance of this Kind.
Their Friends find it a Difficult task to make
them Christians. In the first Place a *Clergyman* ought to be Serious, Wit is Light, and un-
suitable to his Cloth. Wit is nourish'd by
Wine, and Pleasant Conversation. The
Clergyman's business is Sobriety, and Retirement. Wit lies in *Plays*, *Romances*, *No-
vells*, *Lampoons* and other Performances of
that Nature, excepting Balls, Assemblies and
Masquerades. But the *Clergyman's* Employment are the *Bible*, Thirty nine Articles,
Book of Homilies, *Journal of the Convocation*,
Practice of Piety, *whole Duty of Man* &c. And
he ought to shine no where in the way of
Wit, but at a Christning, Wedding, or
some other *Parochial Occasion*, where a *Jejune*
Story of *King Charles* the Second's Days will
not fail of meeting with great Applause.

Formerly the *fair Sex* had very large Pre-
tensions to Wit; but now alas! Modesty
cuts them off: For I cannot think they will
be disposed to purchase that Name at the ex-
pence of their Reputation. The Truth is, I
am very unwilling to exclude them, from
what

what wou'd be a confiderable Addition to the
reft of their fhining *Qualities* ; but the *Ini-
quity* of the Times will have it fo. And I
wifh I cou'd fay that of late they had not
joyn'd in the common Cry againft Wit, and
enter'd into feveral dangerous Combinations
oppofite to that Claim. A *beautiful Face*,
a *fine Shape*, a *gentle Mien*, a *fweet Accent;*
a *graceful Carriage*, and other fuch like Ingre-
dients of a *compleat Lady*, tho' they cannot
be call'd Wit, yet by the *Courtefy* of all Men
of *Wit*, *and Honour*, they entitle the *Pro-
prietors* to the Name and Privileges of *Wit* ;
as being the Natural Confequences of *Wit*,
and *Ingenuity* ; but now all thefe noble
Symptoms of *Femal Merit* are loft under *Farce*,
and *Mafquerade*, we can neither diftinguifh
the Perfections, nor do Juftice to the right
Owner. The *Jilt*, and the *Sincere Lover*, *Beauty*
and *Abomination*, *Virtue* and the *Lady of
Pleafure* are fo blended together, that this
Nation never before countenanc'd fo publick
an Injuftice done to their *Fair Sex*. Yes, they
are now fallen to fuch a State of *Degeneracy*,
that they have put off the very outward Body
of Wit, and taken up an *Apifh Carriage* in
its

its stead. *Affected Accents, Impertinent* Gaity. *unmannerly Wispering, unseasonable Gigling, crumpling* the *Mouth, peeping through the Eye,* with a Thousand such like *Italian Grimaces,* have quite demolish'd the fine *English Lady.* And if there is any remains of *Wit,* yet among them it can only be call'd *Cunning,* in carrying on an I*ntrigue,* which notwithstanding is every Day forfeited by a *Foolish Discovery.*

We are now coming to the *Politick Impediments* of Wit. In these Days few *wise Men* write Books; and *Fools* cannot Write. What a loss of time is it therefore, to read the Works of this *Age?* There are many *Politick Reasons* why a Man shou'd never put Pen to Paper in Quality of an *Author;* but none more prevalent than I*nterest.* If any thing cou'd induce a Man to act against his *Interest* it wou'd be *Wit,* which often Sacrificeth Friends, Relations, and every thing that Dear, and Valuable. Some *witty Fools* there are who rather chuse to Starve than not exercise their *Faculty* contrary to their own *Interest,* but the Generality wou'd gain by their Wit. The Craft of *Booksellers* has occasion'd several of my Acquaintance to ab-

stain

ſtain from being witty, tho' otherwiſe they were well Qualified. Perſons of *Subſtance,* and who are eaſy in their Fortunes are above the drudgery of Wit ; and thoſe who wou'd live by it, drudge without Profit. All this is owing to the *Bookſellers* who Monopolize the *Merchandize.* There is more Skill required in making a Hand of Wit, than in being really witty. It is Obſervable among the *Jockeys at New-market,* that after the Speed of a *Horſe* is blown, all the Advantage he has above a *Jade* depends upon the *Matchmakers* Craft. But if the Speed of a Running Horſe can be kept a Secret, the whole *Meeting* are eaſily bit. If a *Bookſeller* lays hold of a *Wit,* he endeavours to perſwade him he is not ſo; and by this Means the *Author* is his *Bubble* for ſeveral Years, till the *Smugler* grows rich, and the *Wit* writes himſelf into a Goal.

Frequenting *Coffee-Houſes* is a great Obſtacle to *Wit.* You may meet with an *Atheiſt* in one, a *Socinian* in another, a *Tory* in a Third ; but a Wit in none of 'em. I cannot tell what *Coffee-Houſes* were in Sir *Roger Leſtrange's Days.* Now they are the *Nurſery*

D   of

of Indolence, and Sloth. The *Forge* of Lies. The *Blundershop* of the *Irish*; and if they afford any thing like Wit, 'tis all rais'd in a *Hot* Bed, and dies as soon as the Air is let in upon it. In a Word, the last Felicity of a Man of no Consequence is to shine in a *Coffee-House*.

I was once my self designing to set up for a *Wit*; but several things nearly concerning me made me' desist from the *Enterprise*. A *Gentleman* of Experience caution'd me against it, upon these Considerations. If, said he, you have a Mind to Starve in a *Goal*, to be soundly *Cudgll'd*, and make your Exit at *Tyburn*; your ready way is to turn *Wit*. *Wit* and *Poverty* commonly go hand in hand. There are only two ways of Subsisting in this Life. *Trade*, and *Patrimony*. A *Wit* is too much given to *Flights* to be *Industrious*. Speculation is a thin Diet, and few grow Fat upon it. A Moderate *Genius*, *Dutch Capacity*, or *Trafficking Wit* is the only Method to grow rich. Between the *Bookseller* and the *Tavern*, the Wit Starves. He empties his Purse to supply himself with Wit, and the *Bookseller* brings so many Articles of

Discount

Difcount for *Paper, Printing, Advertifements, Publifhing, Stationers-Hall;* befides the Perquifites belonging to the Knavifh Part of the *Calling:* That the *Copy-mony* will fcarce keep the Wit alive, till fome National Folly gives him an opportunity of Recruiting. Few *Wits* give the World any Diverfion after they have Writ themfelves into a *Poft.* A Man that abufes another without Wit, deferves to be Cudgell'd : And he that does it wittily is actually Cudgell'd. Wit in thefe Days, as I obferv'd before is divided in a great Meafure between *Smut,* and *Satyr ;* in both cafes you are in danger of being beaten, upon the firft Occafion the *Ladies* out of Decency, rap you with their Fan, in the latter you run the rifque of a more ferious Chaftifement. But the Confequences of *Wit* are ftill more *dreadful.*

A *Wit* has fometimes a Temptation to become a *Politician.* He is for prying into *State Affairs,* and attacking *Parties ;* in which Cafe he always falls a Sacrifice when the *Power* Shifts.

I have known one *Clergyman* made a *Dean,* and another condemn'd to the *Pillory,* for

the

the very fame piece of Wit well and ill Cal-
culated. Have we not all feen the Prifons
of *London* and *Weftminfter*, crowded with
Wits from the *Lord Treafurer* to the *Cobler
of High-Gate?* *Printers*, *Publifhers*, *Book-
fellers*, *News-writers*, *Ballad-fingers*, and all
fuch *Retailers* of Wit daily hurry'd to an un-
welcome Retirement, are woeful Inftances
of the fmall Encouragement Men have to be
witty. Nay every *Execution Day*, tho' *Tray-
tors*, *Shoplifters*, *High-way-men*, *Houfe-break-
ers* &c. are lamented by their Friends and
Relations upon many other Accounts, yet nothing is fo often repeated as the occafion of
their difmal end, as an excefs of *Wit* and *Ingenuity.*

While I was Entertaining my felf with
thefe Thoughts, an Affertion of Mr. *Whi.—s*
came into my Mind, *vid.* That the late general *Ecclipfe* was a great Occafion of the
Decay of *Wit* in this *Ifland.* The Reafon he
alledg'd was; becaufe it created a certain
Chillnefs in the *Inhabitants* which had never
left them fince, but daily prey'd more and
more upon their natural Warmth, till at laft
it reduced 'em to fuch a State of Stupidity

as

as to be obliged to muffle themselves up in *Masquerade*. But this perhaps may be look'd upon as much a Dream, as to make the *Comet* which appear'd before the Death of King *Charles* the Second, the Occasion of the General *Deluge*. So I leave the *Letter*, and only stick to the M*oral*. A great *Wit* may Ecclipse little Ones so far, as to make the World regardless of them. There has been something of this of late in *Great Britain*. A great *Poet*, a great *Mathematician*, a great *General*, a great *Physician*, a great *Man*, and a great *King*, have made all others respectively insignificant in that Way. Who pretends to talk of Longitude in the Presence of Mr. R——r ? To pronounce boldly upon a Distemper since the death of Dr. R——e, or disturb the Peace of *Europe* when *King George* is the Guarantee of the Worlds Felicity ?

The Success of pretended *Wits* has depriv'd the World of the Blessing of real *Ones*. Nothing can be a greater Discouragement than to see *Trifles* Rewarded, and *Blockheads* carried in Triumph. The Success of very bad *Plays*, has made the best *Poets* turn *Farmers*, and *Stock-jobbers*; nothing discovers

more

more the National Degeneracy as to *Wit*, than to hear the *Theatre* clap at a Sergeant's calling a Country Clown *Gentleman-Soldier*, and sit unconcern'd at a *Period* worth a thousand *Pistoles*. When all other things were vendible, *Wit* cou'd never be purchas'd till of late. Ben *Johnson*, and *Shakespear* never brib'd for Wit. But now a Man is esteem'd either *Fool*, or *Wit*, according as he makes *Friends*, or *Enemies*. A Powerful *Patron* must be engaged by a *Dedication*. The World seduced by the blaze of a *Title*. The Trifle tip'd at both ends with a borrow'd *Prologue*, and *Epilogue*. The *Audience* bespoke from all Corners of the Town, before the Timorous Wit dare expose himself to the Publick. Strip *C---r* of these Advantages, and what will become of the *N---j---r*. *(Cibber) (Konjuroe)*

It is not to be Accounted the least occasion of the Decay of Wit, to be too well acquainted with *Foreign Languages*. This makes a Man a *Wit-hunter* which is no better than a *High-way-man*. The Impiety comes not to a head all on a suddain. It begins in our Youth, with Stealing our Exercise at *School* with capping Verses, and repeating *Hudibras*. Afterwards when we begin to set up for our selves, we

we are so addicted to transposing and transla-
ting, that we are never sure to say any thing of
our own but when we say something that is
dull and insipid. Are not one half of our *Booksellers* Shops fill'd with Foreign Wit? The
Spanish Rogue, the *Italian Politician*, the
German Rapsodist, the *French Novelles*, *Romances* and *Memoirs* are the chief Orna-
ment of every Gentleman's Library. The
Dutch are the only People, who seem to
have very little to complain of us for the
embezelling of Foreign Wit.

Human Respect has a mighty Influence
over our Actions, let them be good or bad.
The State of this Life will not permit us
to be so refin'd in our Motives, as not to
have some Mercenary Views in the Performance of our Duty. This Imperfection
is observable in *Wit*, as well as in other
Things. The Fear of a *Critick* often makes
Men either silent or insipid: This is no
small Source of the Decay of *Wit*: *Bash-
fullness* is equal to *Folly*. There is no Difference as to the Improvement of Mankind,
whether a Person is a *real Fool* or a *dumb
Wit*. 'Tis the Awe the World lives in of

Criticks,

Criticks, which occasioneth this great De-triment. The greatest *Wit* has commonly more Pride than Wit ; and his Pride makes him conceal his Wit, for fear of being hum-bled under a Disappointment. A Man must be an *Impudent Wit* to survive being hiss'd once off the Stage : Hence it is that the most *celebrated Wit* will not venture himself a-broad without the Strong Guard of a *Patron, Preface, Dedication* &c. And very often un-der all these Advantages, an ill Natur'd *Cri-tick* shall trip up his Heels, and the *Pastry Cook* becomes the Heir of his *Lucubrations.* Nor indeed, can any *Wit* be without Fear upon these Occasions. If he is a *Party-man,* he directly challenges one half of the *Nation.* If he affects being *Prudent,* and sets up for a *Neutrality,* he is declar'd Insipid, and pleases no Body. *Writing a Book,* is stripping a Mans self Naked. He that conceals his Sentiments, and Learning may be suppos'd to know more than he really does. But when a *Per-son* Writes, he is suppos'd to write his best, and exhaust himself in the Cause ; and by making the rest of Mankind as wise as him-self he becomes Contemptible.

The

The Death of a *Parent* is an infupportable Lofs to a *Child*, when it is to be expofed to a *hazardous Education*. There is always a *Corps de referve* in an Army to fecure the *Conqueſt* at the latter end of a Day. Some Wits there are which languiſh, unlefs they are well Seconded. The *Ivy* climbs by the ſtrength of the *Oak*; and the Feeble *uncorrect Genius* wants an able Hand to give it a Luſtre. What a poor Figure do *Second Rate Wits*, make when they are left deſtitute by the Death, or Abfence of a *Potent Auxiliary?* When one Wit turns *Secretary* of State, another ceaſeth to be *Secretary* of the *Muſes*. The *Oak* is cut down for the uſe of the *British Navy*, the *Ivy* falls, and is trodden under every Bodies Feet. Thus of late the rewarding of *Real Wits*, has been the ruin of *Pretenders*.

Nothing can be more oppoſite than *Wit* and *Traffick*. When the *bright Men* of a Nation give themſelves to *Stock-jobbing*, they are Inpenetrable to a Jeſt. The beauty of a fine *Period*, and *Numeration Table* have nothing Common. Thoſe who were employed in comparing Antient, and Mo-

E   dern

dern Authors, are now adjusting *Receipts* and *Disbursements*. While the *South Sea Stock* rises so much, Wit will fall Proportionably. And *Gresham-College* can never carry on their Projects of finding Forrests in the Bowels of Acrons, and equipping Fleets to fetch Weeds from the *Indies*, while *Coronets* and *Blew Garters* and such as shou'd contribute towards it, are seen so often at *Change Alley.*

Bad Company is no less dangerous in regard of Morals, than of Wit. *Thieves, Drunkards,* and *Whore-Masters,* are all made by the Force of *Example.* And a *Wit* degenerates by conversing with an unpolish'd *People.* The finest Marble discovers not its beautiful Veins till Art has improved Nature. Some Nations are *Refiners,* other Nations go no farther than a *Fowl-draught.* Some have their *upper Rooms* well Furnish'd, others their *Store-houses.* Frugality is commendable in low Life. But 'tis a hard *Fate* upon a Nation, that Men cannot become Rich without being Blockheads.

But among all the Impediments of Wit, none gives more Disturbance, especially in

a

a *Mercenary Nation*, than that it fhou'd go *unrewarded*, which I fear will be my Fate in this *Pamphlet*. *Baftards* are often made *Dukes*, Whores *Counteffes*, and *Bawds* enrich'd with *Crown Lands*, while the *Wit* is removed from the Stage of Life, without either *Land*, or *Title*. The Sailor is provided for at *Greenwich*. The Soldier at *Chelfea*. But the Wit after he has languifh'd away his Bloom in fruitlefs Attempts of climbing by *Intrinfick Merit*, has no Place to retire to but *Bedlam*; and fo is under a Neceffity of going out of his Wits, becaufe he cou'd not live by 'em.

THE

Dancing Devils:

OR, THE

Roaring Dragon.

A Dumb FARCE.

As it was lately Acted at Both Houses, but particularly at one, with unaccountable Success.

Pray tell me, whether, in a vicious Age,
The Stage corrupts the Town, or Town the Stage?
For both concur, when Folly makes its way;
But where the Fault begins, 'tis hard to say.

Veluti in speculum. —— *Utile dulci.*

LONDON

Printed ; and Sold by A. BETTESWORTH at the *Red-Lion*, J. BATELY at the *Dove*, in *Pater-noster-Row* ; and J. BROTHERTON at the *Bible* in *Cornhil*. MDCCXXIV.

Price One Shilling.

The Dancing Devils :

O R,

The Roaring Dragon, &c.

 NEAR barren Fields, where Honour dwells,

Difgrac'd with rotten Pofts and Rails,

Which long have fenc'd that fpacious Square,

Where Bawds and Bailiffs take the Air,

And crippl'd Rogues, with Fronts of Brafs,

Implore the Aid of all that pafs ;

Where loit'ring Vagabonds, by Day,

Walk, gaze and ftarve their Hours away,

And Bullies wrangle in the Night,

With money'd Rakes that fear to fight ;

A 2 Where

Where Players often take their Turns,

To con their Parts in Summer Morns,

And broken Gamesters strole to meet

Some Cully that will Lend or Treat;

Where neighb'ring Porters reel about,

When gorg'd with *Winchesters* of Stout,

To belch and fizzle out the Stinks

Engender'd by their nauseous Drinks;

Where Butchers often have a Call

To Cricket, Boxing, or Trap-Ball;

And where, when they in Summer curse

The Flies, and sultry Weather worse,

They drop at Night their stinking Veal,

And other Meats too rank for Sale;

Tho' 'tis ill Manners to offend

The Nostrils of their bounteous Friend,

For whom they cock their greasy Beavers, ⎫

Battle their Bludgeons into Shivers,   ⎬

And ring their Marrowbones and Cleavers. ⎭

Near

Near to thefe Fields, as I before
Have faid, and now I fay, *encore,*
There ftands a Fabrick of Renown,
Erected to amufe the Town,
Sometimes with Heroes raving mad
For Love, or fomething elfe as bad ;
Whofe Rants, too oft, perfwade the Fair,
They're greater Witches than they are ;
And that, when any charming Dame
Has in her Champion rais'd a Flame,
Her Frowns, if fh'as a mind to fwagger,
Will wound him deeper than a Dagger.

At other times this famous Pile,
With comick Scenes would make ye Smile,
And fhow bad Hufbands and ill Wives,
Their very Pictures and their Lives,
That each might laugh alike to fee
Themfelves, and take the Stage to be
Their own falacious Family.

This

This House was, also, once defign'd
T'inftruct, as well as pleafe Mankind,
That all degrees of humane Creatures
Might learn their Duty to their Betters,
And, by Examples on the Stage,
Be taught the Manners of the Age,
How Quality fhould be accofted,
And how far Honour might be trufted,
What Courtiers Promifes are binding,
And when their Words are worth the minding.

Here Statefmen fhould, by *Wolfey*'s Fall,
Be caution'd how they grafp at all ;
And learn of *Cecil* how to fteer
The Helm, when threat'ning Storms are near;
What Tools to bribe, what Caufe to prop,
How far to go, and when to ftop ;
For Riders often lofe the Race,
By fetting out too fwift a pace.

Here

Here vicious Governors fhould fee
The dire Effects of Tyranny,
And how proud Fav'rites have been torn
From Kings, and made the Peoples fcorn :
What Vertues reign'd in Ages paft,
When Men were Wife and Women Chaft,
And how whole Kingdoms have been won
By Valour, and by Vice undone :
How Crowns, which purple Seas have coft.
By treach'ry have been gain'd and loft ;
And how Great Men, mifled by Paffions,
Have prov'd the bane of wealthy Nations:
How Beauty, by engaging Arts,
Hath charm'd the moft heroick Hearts,
And made Imperial Rulers wave
Their Scepters to fome female Slave.

 Here all degrees of human Race,
Should fee themfelves, as in a Glafs,
And, by a well-digefted Play,
Be taught to govern and obey.

Here

Here Innocence should see the great
Rewards that do on Vertue wait;
And Libertines, that scoff at Priests,
And make the Holy Text their Jests,
Should in *Don John* behold the fate
Of Princely Rakes, who sin in state,
And prove as Wicked as they're Great.

This also should have been the Seat
Of Language, of Humour and of Wit,
Of Musick, Poetry, and all
The pleasing Arts Theatrical.

Here *Shakespere* to *Elizion* fled,
And, *O rare Ben*, should live, tho' dead,
That their inimitable Plays,
In others, might a Genius raise,
And teach 'em to deserve the Bays.

Here

Here modern Wits, by Art, fhould court
The Favour of the Noble Sort,
And in juft Characters expofe,
Sots, Cowards, Proftitutes and Beaus,
Who langh at Vertue, and defpife
The fober Counfels of the Wife.

But now, the Stage revolts from thefe
Dramatick Rules, that us'd to pleafe,
And does, in fcorn of Wit, impofe
Upon the Town, *Dumb Raree Shows,*
Compos'd of Vizards and Grimaces,
Fine Scenes, Machines, and Antick Dreffes;
As if old Plays were, by the Proud,
Thought too inftructive for the Croud,
Becaufe they fhow, in Ages paft,
How evil Statefmen far'd at laft;
Ought therefore to be quite fufpended,
Until the wicked World is mended,

B   And

And nothing be allow'd to teach
The Town, but Action without Speech,
By Wisemen stil'd, *Dumb foolish Whims*,
But by learn'd Blockheads *Pantomims*.

   Here *Jove* transforms himself, when mad
For Love, into a Horned Pad,
And then, his raging Lust to please,
Bulls fair *Europa* crofs the Seas:
As if our Stage-Projectors meant,
When this *Dumb Op'ra* they prefent,
T'inform us, by their speechless fooling,
How Dames of old, like Cows, lov'd Bulling;
Or, that the Charms one Maid poffeft,
Could change a God into a Beaft.
Why not? since Women oft, we find,
New-mould their Husbands to their Mind,
And Ladies, with their sweeteft Looks,
To Bucks and Rams, turn Lords and Dukes;

                   Nahl

Nah! ride 'em, if they bear the Rule,
As fair *Europa* did her Bull,
And wifely make the Nuptial Craft,
At once their Holdfaft and their Jeft.

   Some damn'd the Bull, upon the Stage,
And thought it gor'd the prefent Age ;
The blufhing Ladies wifh'd it thence,
Thro' Fear the Horns fhould give Offence,
Knowing, by Nuptial Obfervation,
As well as fkilful Penetration,
'That Cuckolds, like Fanatick Meeters,
Are very tender-confcienc'd Creatures,
And always feem much difcontented,
When e'er themfelves are reprefented.
However, now, all horned Brutes
Are laid afide, to pleafe Cornutes,
And, in their room, a Beaft of Prey,
More fierce and terrible than they,

Does

Does from the distant Clouds fly down,
And, roaring, scares the gazing Town;
Not only with his pointed Wings,
His Tail, his Tallons, and his Stings,
But with loud Thunder-claps and Light'ning,
Added to make his Looks more fright'ning.

Therefore, fair Ladies, when you go
To see this sad tremendous Show,
If, by good Luck, you pregnant are,
Take Courage, or at least take care,
This monstrous Enemy to Marriage,
Makes you not quake and spill your Porrage;
For dreadful Sounds and Sights uncommon,
Are dang'rous to a breeding Woman.
But I, in hopes to please you better,
Shall here describe this frightful Creature,
In such a manner as no Bride
May at the sight be terrify'd,
But gaze her fill, and not fear losing
What teeming Ladies gain by 'Spousing.

In

In Ballads and in penny Books,

Oft sung and said in Chimney-Nooks,

There is an ancient Tale, concerning

One *Faustus*, famous for his Learning,

Whose wond'rous Feats, in Times of yore,

At Fairs and Wakes were lyrick'd o'er,

And made the Sport of rural Sinners,

At *Christmas* Feasts and Wedding-Dinners.

Nor was this Doctor fam'd for prating

Of *Hebrew*, Heathen *Greek*, or *Latin*,

Or, for those common Scraps of Knowledge,

By e'ery Dunce pick'd up in College;

But for his depth in Magick Art,

As good old Grand-dames do assert,

By which, when e'er he wav'd his Wand,

He could whole Troops of Dev'ls command,

And make a thousand Imps and Furies,

Dance Minuets, Rigadoons, and Bories;

Force wand'ring Spirits to arise,

And show their Shapes to human Eyes.

Nah!

Nah! by his magick Pow'r, compel
The Dev'l himself, in fpight of Hell,
To fing a Song, when wife Men know
They have no Harmony below,
And that th' infernal Dominator
Loves Mufick next to Holy-Water:
It founds not therefore very well,
That Songfters fhould arife from Hell,
A place where no Muficians dwell.

However, be it falfe or true,
What Books report, and Ballads too,
By all, who would be well contented,
To have thefe Devils reprefented,
Such Wonders may be heard and feen,
At the Great Booth near *Lincolns-Inn*,
As do with Crouds their Benches fill,
Tho' fitter much for *Windmil-Hill*;
Or for the Rounds of *Smithfield*, where
That Lordly Magiftrate the Mayor,

Pro-

Proclaims a Fair in solemn Pomp,
With twenty Catchpoles at his Rump.

Thus, when instead of Wit, we find
Dumb Shows, of an inferior kind,
Fit only for the Approbation
Of Mortals in the lowest Station,
Wherein a huge Sham-Dragon flies,
And dancing Dev'ls in Crouds arise,
The Stage where Poets should delight us,
Is then, become a Hell to fright us.
Nor does this Pile, which heretofore
Was justly deem'd a Theatre,
Deserve, from *Harlequin*'s uncouth
Designs, a better Name than *Booth:*
  For whilst the Lass preserves her Honour,
  We put the style of Maid *upon her,*
  But when corrupted, to her shame,
  We brand her with an odious Name.

At

At this new metamorphos'd Houſe,

Where Hell does very oft break looſe,

And where they've little more to brag on,

Than two good Dev'ls and one huge Dragon,

The fam'd Projector of theſe Shows,

That vex the Wits but pleaſe the Beaus,

Does, by his *Hocus pocus* Art,

Make all the gazing Audience ſtart,

In repreſenting to their view,

The Tricks old *Fauſtus* us'd to ſhew,

Hoping e'relong he ſhall obtain

The with'ring Bays from *Drury-Lane*,

Therefore poor *Harlequin*'s ſo civil,

To ſign a Contract with the Devil,

That the New-Houſe may damn its Rival.

   So envious diſcontented Wretches,

   When deſpicably poor, turn Witches,

   And then on Broomſtaves ride in ſtate,

   To be reveng'd of thoſe they hate.

Thus

Thus *Harlequin*, who long had vied
With *Drury-Lane*, to low'r its Pride,
And puzzl'd his contriving Wits,
To plague his thriving Oppofites,
Labour'd in vain till he became
A Wizard, under *Fauftus* Name,
And then, by th' Pow'r of Necromancy,
He charm'd and tickl'd e'ery Fancy,
From mighty Lords, to City Culls,
And from great Ladies, down to Trulls;
For tho' fome Folks, in thefe good Days,
Like Puritans, may keck at Plays,
Yet they conceive it no Offence,
To fee the Doctor's Devil dance;
And that's the Reafon, I fuppofe,
Why Saints and Sinners, Bels and Beaus,
In crouds, dance aft'r'im, e'ery Night
He's pleas'd to make himfelf a Sight.

Thus far, my rude unpolifh'd Song
Is but a Proem, tho' too long,

C

And

And now my Muſe intends to make

The ſpeechleſs Show of *Fauſtus* ſpake;

That is, in Hudibraſtick Verſe,

He means to lyrick o'er the Farce,

Which, by dumb Action and Grimaces,

Has gull'd ſo many thouſand Aſſes;

But, leſt I ſhould offend the Town,

I freely own myſelf as one.

Excuſe my Muſe, ſhe's forc'd ſometimes,

To uſe ill-natur'd Words for Rhimes,

When really ſhe intends no hurt,

But only Snarls to make you ſport;

As Madam's Lap-Dog does, when.e'er

We kiſs or touch his Lady fair,

Too long I've kept you in ſuſpence,

I doubt, by dull Impertinence;

But now my Muſe has eas'd her Spleen,

She's juſt beginning to begin,

Tho' fears, her Farce will only ſeem,

To Men of Sence, the *Devil's Dream*.

The

The Necromancer:

OR

Harlequin *turn'd Doctor* Fauſtus.

Act I. Scene, *The Doctor's Study.*

THe firſt thing *Harlequin* preſents ye,
  Moſt humbly hoping to content ye,
Is his own Perſon, in the ſhape
Of *Fauſtus*, whom he ſtrives to ape,
But dreſs'd in a Priciſian's Coat,
Or formal Cloak, as if he taught
Some Alley Conventicle, where
The Saints, for good Advice, repair,
Juſt ſuch a Dreſs as, heretofore,
Old *Fauſtus* in his Study wore,
When the poor Conj'rer was ſo civil,
To ſtrike a Bargain with the Devil,
Which made the ſubterranean Prince
Of Darkneſs, love the Garb e'er ſince,

C 2   Ex-

Expecting each fanatick Brother,

Will Sign and Seal some time or other;

Not such as deal in Alms and Pray'rs,

But those Religious Conjurers,

Who, tho' they boast their Gospel-Labours,

Thro' Envy, make it their Endeavours,

To raise the Dev'l among their Neighbours.

As *Harlequin* with sober Looks,

Sits musing near his Shelves of Books,

With his good *Genius* and his bad,

In white and sable Garments clad,

Contending, in harmonious Lays,

To lead the Doctor diff'rent ways,

But thirst of Knowledge makes him chuse

Th'Advice he's caution'd to refuse.

Now from a corner of the Skies,

A strange Epistle downward flies,

And shoots itself, directly plumb,

'Twixt *Harle*'s Finger and his Thumb.

The

The Superfcription of which Letter
Is turn'd tow'rds every Spectator,
That Boxes, Galleries and Pit,
Should fee what Hand the Dev'l had writ,
Which, to each curious Eye, appears
As grand as a Commiffioner's,
Who, when he Signs, will let us fee
He fcribbles by Authority.

But tell me, Criticks, if you pleafe,
You that are fkill'd in Niceties,
Why does this Letter from above
Fly down, as if it came from *Jove ?*
When fome young trap-door Imp, from Hell,
Might have deliver'd it as well;
For what's directed from the Clouds,
Seems to be fent us by the Gods;
But what th'Infernal Prince difpatches,
To Wizards, Conjurers, or Witches,
Should upwards be convey'd, to fhow,
'Twas Hocus'd pocus'd from below;

Tho'

Tho' this their Advocates may fay,

That the Poft-Dev'l miftook his Way.

But that Excufe is next to none,

Since Doctor *Harlequin* muft own,

There's not an Imp the Dev'l efpoufes,

Or tempting Fiend that Hell produces,

But knows the Road to both the Houfes.

  Therefore the Reafon to be given,

Why the Scrowl drops, as if from Heaven,

Muft be our Conjurer's defire

To fhew what Magick lies in Wire,

By th' Pow'r of which, we do fuppofe,

All Puppits move in Puppit-Shows,

Leap, tumble, dance like little Fairies,

And play a thoufand ftrange Figaries,

Which oft delude the fond Spectators,

To vow and fwear they're living Creatures.

Why then fhould fuch ingenious Arts

Be ridicul'd by Men of Parts?

When

When us'd with Judgment to surprize
Great Persons, most profoundly wise.

 O vain attempt! to thus impose
On Lords and Ladies, Wits and Beaus,
When, by the way, tho' Juglers Tricks
May puzzle Fools and Country Hicks,
Yet wiser Heads discern the Cheat,
And, scoffing, laugh at the Deceit.

 The Dev'l, who has more Traps to take us,
Than Mouse-trap-builder e'er could make us,
Exhibits, now, Bait after Bait,
T'entice the Doctor to his Net,
Sings like an Angel to allure him,
But can't, as yet, in Bonds secure him;
Tempts him with e'ery worldly Good,
To sign the Contract with his Blood,
Lays him down Crowns and Scepters too,
But still the Dev'l a bit 'twill do.
At last, by means of some Adviser,
His sable Highness growing wiser,

Re-

Refolv'd to introduce fo fweet,

So fine, fo charming a Deceit,

That Flefh and Blood, tho' ne'er fo cautious'

Should not withftand a Bait fo lufheous.

And what d'ye think this ftrange uncommon

Expedient prov'd to be, but Woman,

A tempting Dev'l in *Helen*'s Shape,

On whom made a Rape;

And by his vile adult'rous action

Brought *Ilium* into fad diftraction:

Accordingly up ftarts the Shade

Of this alluring pritty Jade,

With Face fo fair, and Eyes fo bright,

Her Breafts fo round, her Skin fo white,

Her Hips fo plump, her Wafte fo fmall,

Her Looks fo Angel-like withal,

That not a gazing Saint or Sinner,

Could guefs fhe had the Devil in her;

Nor had this lovely *Grecian* Ghoft

Alone thefe foothing Charms to boaft,

But

But fung fo fweetly to entice
The Doctor's Ears, as well as Eyes,
That he was all on fire to board her,
As foon as e'er he'ad feen and heard her,
But that the Devil, who watch'd the Water
Of his new fine bewitching Daughter,
Step'd in between, and would not fuffer
What *Fauftus* was about
Or elfe the Doctor would have try'd
Whether his new intended Bride,
Had been equip'd, like other Laffes,
With Flefh and Blood, for Man's Embraces.

Now after all the fruitlefs Baits,
The Wiles, the Traps, the Snares, the Nets,
That *Maferftofiles* had try'd,
Aud *Harlequin* as oft defy'd,
This laft Temptation was fo bright,
That Reafon ftagger'd at the fight;

D   And

And as that great Director fail'd,
The Dev'l and all his Works prevail'd.
So that poor *Fauſtus* now was ready
To ſign and ſeal, for one ſweet Play-day
With this fine Viſionary Lady.

   Thus Beauty, tho' it's all but Air,
A gloſſy Shade that decks the Fair,
Yet wiſer ~~man cannot~~ ſecure
His Breaſt againſt that fatal Lure,
But when he's tempted flies in haſte,
To graſp what proves his bane at laſt;
For ſo our *Zany-Fauſtus* far'd,
When beauteous *Helen*'s Shade appear'd,
And with her Charms ſo ſtruck his Heart,
In ſpight of all his magick Art,
That he, like other am'rous Fools,
Broke thro', at once, weak Reaſon's Rules,
And yielding to the fair Temptation,
In hopes to gratify his Paſſion,
Both ſign'd and ſeal'd his own Damnation.

From

From hence, we learn what Love will make
Poor Lovers do, for Beauty's fake,
Whofe Pow'r no Mortal can withftand,
Till Age has gain'd the upper-hand.

No fooner had the Doctor fign'd
His Contract to the Devil's Mind,
Upon Condition to enjoy
The Fair One who had ruin'd *Troy*,
But running with extended Arms
To take poffeffion of her Charms,
Young *Helen*, like a jilting Minx,
From his Embraces downwards finks,
And when poor *Fauftus* would have kifs'd her,
Up ftarts old *Belzebub*'s own Sifter,
An ugly Hag, as lean and frightful
As *Envy*, and her Looks as fpightful,
So defpicably poor and thin,
As if her Food had only been
Tobacco Quids and Royal Gin.

Thus

Thus he that's fond, to an Excefs,
Of painted Looks and gaudy Drefs,
May fancy his alluring Bride,
An Angel in her wedding Pride,
But when the Damfel's unattir'd,
The Beauty's fled that he admir'd;
And he that chofe her for her Charms,
May find the Devil in his Arms.

The Doctor now thought very ftrange
Of this prepoft'rous fudden Change,
And ftood a while in fuch furprife,
That he could fcarce believe his Eyes,
But found, as moft Men do, too late,
His am'rous Folly and his Fate,
And that the Dev'l had quite undone him,
By putting this damn'd Trick upon him;
Therefore refolv'd to triumph o'er
Th'Infernals, by his magick Pow'r,
And make 'em fervile for the time
Agreed upon, 'twixt them and him,

Almoft

Almoſt forgetting to condole
The loſs of his immortal Soul,
Which pleas'd the Dev'l ſo wondrous well,
He laugh'd three times, and ſunk to Hell.

Fauſtus, of *Helen* thus bereft,
In mournful Solitude is left,
And to his Books does now repair,
In hopes to find ſome Comfort there,
Striking a Folio with his Wand,
And down it drops into his Hand,
O'er which he muſing ſits a while,
Reflecting on the Devil's Guile.

Thus he that's guided by his Luſt,
Does to a dang'rous Pilot truſt,
Who ſhows him oft the pleaſing Strand,
Or wiſh'd for Shore that's near at hand,
But drowns him e're he gains the Land.

The End of the Firſt Act.

Act

Act II.   Scene, *The Doctor's House.*

'TWas now about the Ides of *June*,
   When Men and Maids together run,
With Forks and Rakes to spend the Day
In rural Sports and making Hay,
That *Faustus* first began to shew
The Wonders he had pow'r to do,
Resolving now to make some Sport,
And lead a merry-Life, tho' short;
Accordingly, as half a Score
Brisk Lads and Lasses pass'd his Door,
All dancing in a merry Mood,
Tow'rds Fields adjacent to a Wood,
The Doctor, by his Art, well knowing
Which way the *Nymphs* and *Swains* were going
Soon follow'd, bearing in his Hand
That pow'rful Staff, his Conj'ring Wand,
Without the skilful use of which
No Dev'l would e'er rise off his Breech,

                                    But

But all, like lazy Louts, withstand
The Doctor's positive Command.

So stubborn School-boys ne'er apply
To Book, except the Rod be nigh.
Nor will the Jade that's resty, stir,
Without the use of Whip or Spur.

[*Scene a Hay-Catr in a Meadow surrounded*
by a Wood.]

The Doctor now, with nimble Heels,
Ent'ring the fertile Meads and Fields,
Found some at Work, some full of Play,
Some carting, others cocking Hay,
Some lazing on the shady Banks,
Some telling Tales, some playing Pranks,
Some hungry Clowns dispos'd to guttle,
Some sucking at the Leathern Bottle,
Whilst those that thought a *Whet no let*,
Did to their Scythes new edges set,
And lavish'd half their time in fidd'ling
About their Tools, to cloak their id'ling.

As

As Lawyers Clerks, who hate much pains,
Neglectful of their Master's Gains,
Instead of minding Bonds or Leases,
Sit whitt'ling useful Pens to pieces.

The Doctor having now a fancy
To exercise his Necromancy,
Strikes with his magick Wand the Ground,
And strait is heard a pleasing Sound,
The Lads and Lasses rowl their Eyes
Around the Fields in great surprise,
Unable to discover whence
Arose these sweet melodious Strains,
No blind Crowdero, lame and old,
Or piping Swain, could they behold,
No Fidlers stroling to a Fair,
Or Barber, with his Citern, there;
Yet with the Musick which they heard,
They were at once both pleas'd and scar'd.

Like Dam'sels ripe for Generation,
Ravish'd 'twixt Force and Inclination.
Faustus

Fauftus obferving fome delighted,
And others with his Mufick frighted,
Refolv'd, before the Rufticks parted,
To make the gaping Crew light-hearted;
Accordingly, with awful hand,
He waves his diabolick Wand,
And by his Pow'r compels 'em all
To dance as at a Buttock-Ball,
Where Belly-Bobs give no diftafte,
But Rudenefs paffes for a Jeft,
And e'ery clofe indecent Squeefe,
Betwixt the Navel and the Knees,
Are only taken by the Fair,
To fignify the Love you bear.

When, for fome time, the Revel-Rout
Had frifk'd their nimble Tails about,
The Doctor, willing to conclude
This merry hoid'ning Interlude,
Circles his magick Sceptre round
And round, upon the inchanted Ground,

E   Till

Till by the Motions of his Rod,
With now and then a Stamp or Nod,
He does the Clowns together mufter,
And makes 'em dance into a Clufter;
Then, as directed by the Spell,
They hobble out, fo fare 'em well.

    Thus when the Dev'l, as here 'tis fhewn us,
    Has got an ugly bank upon us,
    Our Bodies and our Minds he teafes,
    And makes us do what e'er he pleafes.
    Therefore, ye Clowns, from hence take warning,
    And fay your Pray'rs both Night and Morning,
    Then can no Fairies pinch your Arms,
    Or Wizards plague ye with their Charms,
    No Hags beftride you in your Beds,
    And gallup ye like Hackney Jades,
    At Midnight, thro' the mifty Air,
    O'er Hills and Steeples, G— knows where,
    But, as your good old Grandames fay,
    You may defy, if you but pray,

                                 All

All magick Spells, or Witches pride,
The Dev'l and all his Works beside.

Scene, *The Doctor's House.*

The Doctor, having play'd his Tricks
Among the Jugs and Country Hicks,
Does to his Mansion-House repair,
T'attend his Fortune-telling there.
No sooner is the Wizard come,
From the adjacent Meadows, home,
But two young merry Jades make bold,
And knock, to have their Fortunes told.
The Doctor's Man, as arch a Knave
As any Conjurer need have,
Opens the Door with humble Mein,
And, bowing low, invites 'em in.

Scene, *The Doctor's Study.*

Then leads 'em to the Study, where
They silently sit down and stare

E 2   At

At the Books, Globes, and Allegators,
Huge Snakes, and other monftrous Creatures,
Us'd by moft Emp'ricks to delight,
Or rather to amufe the fight
Of the poor Fools they mean to bite.

 Thus *Fauftus* makes the Maidens wait
A little while, in point of State,
At length approaches, and to fhow
His College-Breeding, bows full low,

 For you muft know, that artful Men
 Can bend in e'ery part for Gain,
 Yet ftill the pride of Heart retain.

The Doctor thus falutes the Laffes,
But not a Word between 'em paffes;
For Scholars vers'd in magick Art,
By Signs, their Sentiments impart,
And can another's Meaning reach,
By gaping, better than by Speech.

 So the Free-Mafons have a way,
 By private Signals, to convey

       Their

Their secret Minds to one another,
And can at once command a Brother,
To quit his Scaffold and descend
The Ladder, to salute his Friend ;
And this they do, as Fame records,
Without the needless sound of Words,
Which makes th' illnatur'd World conjecture,
(Instead of useful Architecture)
They, in Ars Magic, *have some dealing,*
And with the Dev'l a fellow-feeling ;
For Secrets by such numbers held,
Must be suspected, whilst conceal'd,
Because, if good, they'd be reveal'd.

   Faustus, who is, among the rest,
As free a Mason as the best,
Having thus giv'n, by dumb Expression,
The Maids a silent Salutation,
Now importunes 'em, by a Sign,
To eat, and drink a Glass of Wine,

                   The

The Damsels freely condescend,

And, *No, I thank you, Sir*, suspend;

The Doctor then lifts up his Hand,

And strikes the Wainscot with his Wand;

Upon which Signal out there starts

A Table, spread with Fowls and Tarts;

Also a Sideboard fill'd with Glasses,

And Wine to entertain the Lasses,

All conjur'd in with so much haste,

T'amuse the Eye and please the Taste,

As if the Dev'l, give him his due,

Had been both Cook and Butler too;

For *Br----n*, whose bus'ness 'tis to please

Rich Beaus with costly Frigasies,

In twice the time, was never able

To furnish out so nice a Table.

   The Maids now eat and drink their fill,

As rural hungry Stomachs will,

Not thinking that the Doctor's Feast

Had been in Satan's Kitchen dress'd,

But

But fed like any Farmer's Daughters,
Suspecting nothing of such Matters;
For had they known by whose kind Aid
Their Banquet had been thus convey'd,
And that Old *Nick* had cook'd the Treat,
Perhaps, in spight, the Dev'l a Bit
The squeamish Gossips would have eat.

 Loud knocking at the Doctor's Door,
Is now repeated o'er and o'er:
At length two tumbling Knaves, truss'd up
In Trunks, like Dancers on the Rope,
Are gravely introduc'd, to show
Their Palms, that they their Fates may know.

 For Conjurers, who Fortunes tell,
Altho' their Cunning is from Hell,
Yet they pretend to Laws and Rules,
By which they cheat believing Fools,
And oft perswade 'em to agree,
That they can future Chance foresee,
By Planets, Moles, or Palmestry.

A^{c-}

Accordingly the Doctor looks
Upon their Hands as Nature's Books,
Examines e'ery Line or Streak,
Tho' harder to be read than *Greek*;
At length, difcovers in their Palms,
Carts, Gibbets, penitential Pfalms,
Ropes, Nofegays, Pray'r-Books, and a Rout
Of gazing Rabble round about,
The Hangman and a guard of Ruffians,
Lamenting Whores, coach'd up with Coffins,
And all the Marks that could portend
A finful Life and fhameful End:
Then thinking he by Art had read
What Satan thus had put in's Head,
By Signs, he makes the Tumblers know,
The Rope would prove their overthrow:
They, fearlefs of their Fate, defpife
The Doctor and their Deftinies,
And fo concluding not to pay
Their Fees, they laughing fkip away.

The

The Wizard, vexing to behold
Himself and Art thus ridicul'd,
Now shakes his Wand with Indignation,
And brings 'em back by Conjuration,
Dancing upon their Hands and Heads,
To further entertain the Maids:
Thus plagues the Rogues, 'till meer Compassion
Makes him revoke his Incantation,
And then away the Vagrants scour,
Like Light'ning, from the Doctor's Door,
Dreading what they despis'd before.

So Orchard-Thieves, as Grandames tell,
Encompass'd by a Midnight Spell,
When early Day-light has dissolv'd
The Charm by which they were involv'd,
Run home more wild than Forest Horses;
As if Old Nick was at their Arses.
From whence all Mortals may deduce
This exc'lent Rule, of wond'rous use;

F   Which

Which is, *Who values peaceful Hours,*
Muſt ne'er offend Superior Pow'rs.
Whether deriv'd from Good or Evil,
'Tis always ſafe, as well as civil, }
To hold a Candle to the Devil.

   The Doctor now his *Exit* makes,
And with him both the Laſſes takes :
No ſooner has he turn'd his Back
Upon the Claret and the Sac,
But the arch Man, behind his Maſter,
Reſolves to make himſelf a Taſter;
Accordingly he goes about
To fill a thumping Bumper out;
But *Fauſtus* cheats him, in a Joke,
And turns the Wine to Fire and Smoke,
From whence ſuch helliſh Fumes aroſe,
As gave Offence to e'ery Noſe,
Touchiug the Senſe ſo piping hot,
That e'ery grave Fanatick thought
He ſmelt a ſecond Powder-Plot. }

                                   This

This artful piece of Conjuration,
This pritty witty Tranfmutation,
Commands an Upper-Gallery Laugh,
The while, Pilgarlick marches off.

    Thus many things, we find, will flip
    As Proverb fays, 'twixt Cup and Lip :
    Nothing is fure i'th' courfe of Fortune,
    But Death and Taxes, they are certain.

Scene, *a Windmil.*

The Miller's Wife now fteps, by chance,
Down from the Mill to take a Dance ;
By chance, we fay, becaufe we know
There's not one Motive in the Show,
That could induce her to become
So merry by herfelf at Home,
Except the Goffip meant, for eafe,
To fhake off her tormenting Fleas,
Thofe Plagues that fkip from Breaft to Breaft,
And feaft, where Man is glad to tafte.

The

The Miller, who abroad had been,

To take a Cup of Ale or Gin,

Returns, does to his Mill repair,

But finds no trusty Helpmate there ;

Comes down and spies the airy Jade

Frisking her Tail about like mad.

The Miller, pleas'd to see her Humour,

Chimes in and dances with his Gammar :

Now both their Heels were so employ'd,

And tost about, as if they try'd

Who was the nimblest, who the strongest,

And which o'th' two could dance the longest ;

Just as they do at Fairs and Wakes,

When Smocks or Gloves are made the Stakes.

At length their active Legs and Thighs,

B'ing weary of this exercise,

They kiss, when they have danc'd their fill,

And trip the Stairs into the Mill,

As if their Inclinations stood

To sweeter Pastimes, full as good,

To please the Limbs and stir the Blood.

So

So rakish Beaus and buxom Jades,

At Buttock-Balls and Masquerades,

First dance, and then away they move

In couples, to refresh their Love.

The Doctor in his hand now takes

A Letter, and his entry makes,

Calls down the Miller from his Dame,

To send the Bumpkin with the same.

The Miller, fearing to offend,

Does at the Doctor's Beck descend,

And after many Points and Signs,

Receives, and Pockets up the Lines;

But still, thro' Dulness, could not find

The Place to which they were consign'd.

The Doctor huffs and struts about,

The Miller then begins to flout,

And sucks his horny Thumbs, to show

He will not of the Errand go;

The Doctor, angry with the Looby,

To find him such a sullen Booby,

Strikes

Strikes up his Heels, and turns the Clown
Upon his brawny Buttocks, down:
The Miller, whose impatient Rump
Grew angry at this mortal Thump,
Starts up, and with his mealy Cap,
Gives *Harlequin* a dusty flap,
Which sets the Conjurer a sneezing,
And to his Eyes proves very teasing.
This pretty Jest, in which does shine,
So much Contrivance and Design,
Does such a Laugh and Clap command,
From e'ery Mouth and e'ery Hand,
As if our brightest Wits had been
Projectors of this wondrous Scene;
Tho' some ill-natur'd carping Fools,
Unskill'd in new Dramatick Rules,
Suspect the Author stole the whole
From some old Merry-Andrew's Droll,
Contriv'd to make the Rabble laugh,
And push his Master's Packets off.

But

But Quality, in this bright Age,

Thofe awful Judges of the Stage,

On whofe dread Looks, as Poets fay,

Depends the Fate of e'ery Play,

May, furely, if themfelves think fit,

Applaud what's neither Senfe nor Wit,

And for their own Diverfion chufe

Dumb Action, fuch as Monkeys ufe.

The Doctor, having loft fair *Helen*,

Now wants to have a fellow-feeling

With buxom *Joan*, the Miller's Wife,

And only darling of his Life;

Accordingly, to gain his Will,

Upftairs he runs into the Mill,

And at the Window finds the Dame,

With whom he hop'd to quench his Flame,

There gives her Earneft, in a few

Sweet Kiffes, what he meant to do.

The Miller, looking upwards, fees him

About fuch Work as did not pleafe him,

Then

Then mounts the Mill, with jealous Heart
And nimble Heels, to spoil their Sport,
But running to the Window where
He'ad seen the Doctor and his Dear;
From thence they undiscover'd creep,
And at another op'ning peep.
The Miller, growing now as full
Of Fury as a jealous Bull,
Takes it, by what he'ad seen, for granted,
His Horns were planting, if not planted:
And thus enrag'd, Revenge he vows,
Upon his Rival and his 'Spouse:
But Doctor *Harlequin*, to fly
The Danger that appear'd so nigh,
Climbs the out Cornish of the Mill,
But angry *Ralph* persues him still,
And round they run, like Rats when Sporting,
Or Rival-Boar-Cats when they're courting,
Endang'ring, by a Trip or Stumble,
Their Necks, at least an ugly Tumble,

That

That muſt have cool'd the heat of Youth,
And laid the Courage of them both.

   But Lovers ſeldom fear their Lives,
   When Woman draws and Fancy drives.

   Now *Harlequin*, with giddy Crown,
Forſakes his rounding and comes down,
The Miller after him, as faſt.
As ſweet Revenge could give him haſt ;
Both eager, one to ſhun his Fate,
Which t'other hop'd to perpetrate ;
But *Harlequin*, whoſe Heels had ſtill
The ſtart of him that own'd the Mill,
Now climbs the Shrowds unto the top,
And leaves the Cuckold ſtaring up :
But headſtrong Jealouſy, that fears
No Female Traps or Rival's Snares,
Still ſpurs and urges him to chaſe
His nimble Foe, from Place to Place,
Who ſtands aloft, and with his Laughter,
Teaſes and dares him to come after :

            G   The

The Miller highly vex'd hereat,

Begins to climb like any Cat;

Which *Harlequin* no sooner sees,

But jumping quits the Shrowds with ease;

And having now again recourse

To his old Art, does, by the force

Of Magick, whirl about the Sail,

As fast as if it blow'd a Gale:

The Miller clinging close, thro' fear

He should be toss'd the L---d knows where,

Cries out aloud for help, but none

Can stop his Wings from flying on.

The Wife comes running down in haste,

Beholds the Sight, and looks aghast,

Stands trembling, whilst her Looby flies,

With Heels now pointing tow'rds the Skies,

Which then again, in half the round,

Are turn'd near Neighbours to the Ground.

This merry Whimsy does obtain

A Laugh from all Degrees of Men;

And

And when they laugh, you may be fure
The Women never look demure.

A Sack of Grain, which had before
Been planted near the Miller's Door,
In order, as we may fuppofe,
For grinding, when the Wind arofe,
Now takes a fudden ftrange Figary,
And fkips and dances like a Fairy:
A rare Conceit, the World muft own,
To pleafe the Humour of the Town:

For it muft needs delight the Eye,
To fee a Sack of Wheat or Rye
So merry, when it's tax'd fo high.

The Conjurer, who thus had teas'd
Poor *Ralph*, and his own Fancy pleas'd,
Now flides away, concludes the Jeft,
And leaves the flying Sails to reft.
The Miller's Man, amaz'd to fee
His Mafter in this Jeopardy,

But

But finding that the Shrowds inclin'd
To flack their pace, for want of Wind,
Now lends a hand in time of need,
That does at once obftruct their fpeed,
And, like a kind good-natur'd Clown,
Helps his poor giddy Mafter down,
Depriv'd of Senfe by panick Fear,
And drunk with Motion and with Air,
Who, at firft Landing, reels about,
As if o'ercome with Ale or Stout,
And belches out the fwallow'd Wind,
Not only upwards, but behind,
Till, by degrees, poor *Ralpho* gains
His Legs and reconciles his Brains;
Which he'as no fooner done, but in
Again comes merry *Harlequin*,
Difguis'd like an odd looking Fellow,
I'th' fhape of a huge Punchionello,
With artificial Head and Hat
Fix'd o'er his own unlucky Pate,

And

And two false Arms upon his Shoulders,

To cheat the Eyes of the Beholders,

A wonderful surprising Piece

Of Art, unknown to *Rome* or *Greece*,

Contriv'd upon this grand Occasion,

To gain the House a Reputation.

For when our Players please the tast

Of Fools, they always thrive the best :

The wiser few are sorry Friends,

The Stage upon the Crowd depends,

They raise the Pence, and by their Praise

Direct that Fools-cap call'd, the Baies.

Therefore no wonder Wit should fail,

And idle Whims succeed so well,

Since in these Times we may discern

Men love to laugh, and not to learn.

Punch nimbly dances to and fro,

His great activity to show,

And with distorted Back and Breast

Makes e'ery Step he takes, a Jest;

But

But had the Butterfly been there,
Which always fhould with Punch appear,
The Lords and Ladies muft have hurt
Their Sides with laughing at the Sport.
But fince the Butterfly was miffing,
Which made the Show not half fo pleafing,
They fhou'd have turn'd their *Claps* to *Hiffing*

The Miller and his trufty Fellow,
Stood gaping now at Punchionello.
At length, for Reafons good, furmis'd,
That Punch was *Harlequin* difguis'd,
The very Knave that had of late
So plagu'd him and defil'd his Mate,
Therefore refolv'd to have his Blood,
Or at leaft cripple him, if he cou'd;
The Clowns accordingly advancing,
Seize Punchionello as he's dancing,
And, without Mercy, drawing out
Their ftick-pig Knives to cut his Throat,

Per-

Perſue their Rage, and with a jirk
Whip off his Head, to make ſure work.
Punch troubles not his Brains about it,
But dances full as well without it :
Th'Aſſaſſins both ſeem greatly frighted,
But the Spectators much delighted :
Twas very pritty, all Folks ſaid,
To ſee Punch dance without his Head,
And keep true Time when's Ears were gone,
As well as if he'ad had 'em on.
The Miller and his Man ſtood quite
Confounded at ſo odd a ſight,
At laſt take courage and agree,
Once more t'attack their Enemy ;
And now, whilſt their Revenge is warm,
Each Ruffain amputates an Arm,
And in a Fury toſſes by
The ſame, where they neglected ly,
Punch keeps on dancing, not regarding
The loſs of Head or Arms a Farthing,

But

But feems as brifk to the Beholders,
As if they ftill were on his Shoulders,
Tho' numbers ftood amaz'd and faid,
'Twas ftrange, in all the Steps he made,
His Heels fhould never mifs his Head.

His cruel Foes perplex'd to fee
This long furviving Prodigy,
Once more refolve to have his Blood,
And rip his Guts out, if they cou'd;
Accordingly, a third Eſſay
They make, to take his Life away;
But as the Clowns are cutting ope
Poor Punch, to let his Garbiſh drop,
Out fkuttles *Harlequin*, and faves
His Intrails from the bloody Knaves:
Thus flies their Rage, as quick as Wind,
And leaves his mangl'd Cafe behind.
The frighted Miller claws his Ears,
His Man, worfe gally'd, gapes and ftares,

Both

Both looking as profoundly filly,

As Tipftaff, Conftable, or Baily,

When to their Scandal and their Coft,

They have fome fcuffling Pris'ner loft.

  Exceffive Claps, profufely loud,

Were now moft lavifhly beftow'd.

No wonder, for what Tongue could hifs

At fuch a grand Device as this?

Not only worthy of the Smiles

Of thofe that rule the *Britifh* Ifles,

But e'ery Mortal that delights,

In Raree-Shows and pritty Sights,

  Next, to compleat this artful Scene,

Aloft appears a fine Machine,

A Chariot, fuch as Play-houfe Gods

Oft take a turn in thro' the Clouds,

When they defcend near Earth, to know

How merry Mortals live below,

Upon the flying Horfe or Mare,

That whirls this Chariot thro' the Air,

The

The Miller and his Man *Lol-poop*,

Sit highly mounted, Cock-a-hoop,

And in the Body of the Machine,

The Miller's Wife and *Harlequin*,

He toying, fhe as ripe for Jading,

As if juft come from Mafquerading ;

And thus the Rivals, who, of late,

Were greater Foes than Dog and Cat,

Now ride aloft, 'twixt Earth and Sky,

As Witches do on Hurdles fly,

And after all their fnarling Ruffles,

Revengeful Broils and bloody Scuffles,

They in a Moment feem to be

In perfect Love and Amity ;

So, without further jealous Feuds,

The Scene, *in nubibus*, concludes.

 Hereby we fee how Men that dread

 The fcandal of a forked Head,

 Blufter like Bullies, to fecure

 Their Wives from any loofe Amour;

But

But when, by chance, they shall discover
The thing they fear'd is done and over,
Their Courage flags, and they become
Obedient Slaves to Cuckoldom,
Fondle their Wives, like tame Wiseakers.
And fawn upon their Cuckoldmakers.

Act III.   Scene, *The Doctor's House.*

NOw *Faustus* having gain'd renown,
    In e'ery neighb'ring School and Town,
For thus reducing to obedience
The Dev'l and all his airy Legions,
Some learn'd Collegiats have a Fancy
To pry into his Necromancy,
And see by what strange Conjuration,
He'ad merited such Reputation,

Accordingly, in Scholars-Gowns

And Trenchard-Caps upon their Crowns,

They knock at *Fauſtus* Gate, and gain

Admittance by the Doctor's Man;

Apologies they ſeem to make,

By Signs, but not a Word they ſpeak;

Which to an Audience from the City,

Seems wondrous Fine, prodigious Pritty,

Becauſe they give, as it appears,

Their Eyes the pref'rence of their Ears,

And wave their Intellects to fix

Their minds on *bocus pocus* Tricks

   The Scholars being uſher'd in,

To Doctor *Fauſtus Harlequin,*

Find ſeveral other Gownmen there,

Converſing with the Conjurer;

For Students touch'd with Melancholick,

Are prone to Myſteries Diabolick,

                        And

And love to talk with Men that know
The Secrets of the Pow'rs below,
Who by infernal Arts can bring
The Dev'l to follow 'm in a String,
And, *Hibre Bifke*, make him Shew
What ever Tricks they bid him do.

   The Scholars having humbly paid
Their filent Compliment, and made
A tacit Signal, that expreft
A dumb but mannerly Requeft,
That the learn'd Doctor would impart,
A Spec'men of his Magick Art.
In anfwer, *Fauftus* fignifies,
By courteous Signs, that he complies;
Accordingly he ftrikes his Wand
Againft the Ground, and does command,
The Shades of *Hero* and *Leander*,
To crofs the *Styx* and hither wander,
A ftrange long Journey from below:
But if the Reader wants to know

Th'im-

Th'important Bus'nefs they have here,

I'll tell him why they do appear;

Thefe Lovers who had long been drown'd,

Tho' living now upon dry Ground,

Are conjur'd from *Elyfium* hither,

To chant a doleful Song together,

In the fine new familiar way

Of Singing, as a Man may fay;

'Tis true, Old *Charon* Acts his part,

And Sings a Ballad with fome Art,

Wherein he proves that *Thunder*, *Plunder*,

And *Wonder*, gingle well with *Blunder*;

Yet without Scandal to the reft,

Of all their Devils *D----k's* the beft,

Who has acquir'd, by Time, and Study,

The nack of pleafing e'ery Body;

A happy Talent, which the Great,

That Rule in Pomp and Ride in State,

Could never boaft------except of late.

The

The Lovers having-fung their Song,
Not fhort and fweet, but dull and long,
Soon vanifh'd from this groffer Air,
To live in Blifs, we know not where
Charon attending in his Poft
To ferry 'm to the happy Coaft,
A Paradife, or place of Joy,
To which departed Spirits fly,
But ne'er poffefs'd until we Die.

Now Ladies, you that have been bedded
By trufty Friends, or fairly wedded,
If powerful Love's prolifick Dart
Has touch'd you in a tender Part,
Pray fortify the fruits of Marriage,
And all ftol'n Leaps, againft Mifcarriage,
That what I fhall defcribe, to pleafe ye,
May make no pregnant Dame uneafy;
For lo, a Monfter next appears,
Not feen till now, this Thoufand Years,

As

As big and long from Teeth to Tail,
As *Trojan* Horfe or *Greenland* Whale,
And at one Meal can fwallow down
A Church, or little Country Town,
Provided neither are too large
For his extenfive Throat to gorge:
No fam'd St. *George*, or *Moor* of *Effex*,
Thofe Valiant Champions for the She-fex,
E'er kill'd, to fave fair Maids or Wives,
A Beaft like this, in all their Lives;
For Serpents in thofe early Days,
WhenStout Knight-Errants fought for Praife,
Were not much bigger than a Horfe,
Poor weakly Creatures ftarv'd at Nurfe,
But the bare Head of our Proud Dragon,
Were it cut off, would load a Waggon;
And when he gapes, his Mouth may par
With *Ludgate*, or with *Temple-bar*;
His glaring Rainbow-colour'd Eyes
Give all Spectators great Surprife,

And

And fhine as dazl'ing in the Night,
As any new-rub'd Convex-light:
His Wings, a due proportion bear,
As Sails do to a Man of War,
And thro' the' Air convey the Creature,
As t'other does the Ship thro' Water:
His fcaly Tail, that's twifted round,
To fave it from the dufty Ground,
Stands always ready cock'd, to Dart
His Sting into a Gyant's Heart,
Or fturdy Knight, that fhould attack
His Rump, or flinch behind his Back.
For Dragons fierce like Women frail
Bear venom both in Tongue and Tail,
And if one End can't Execute
Revenge, they'll make the other do't:
His clumfy Legs, which are no more
Than two behind and two before,
On which he crawls fometimes for Eafe,
Are hollow, like old trunks of Trees:
And in his huge Surprifing Heels
Four dancing Devil's he conceals;

J   Which

Which active Spirits, once a Day,
He sends abroad to seek his Prey,
As hungry *Lyons* do *Jackalls*,
To hunt down other Animals.

In this Condition, does appear
Old *Draco*, hov'ring in the Air,
Till by degrees he does descend,
The Doctor's Fun'ral to attend;
Then from his Legs four Devils start,
And e'ery Demon, plays his Part,
With other Spirits conjur'd in,
To highten this amusing Scene,
And make the Doctor's last Farewel,
To humane Eyes, more terrible.

So the poor Convict, when he's drawn
Thro' London Streets to Paddington,
The greater Croud surrounds the Tree,
More solemn and more sad must be
The dying Rogue's Catastrophe.

Now up and down the Devils frisk,
And e'ery Fiend seems wond'rous brisk,

As

As if they waited for the Ghoſt
Of ſome great Man from ſome high Poſt,
Who when alive had been the bane
Of thouſands, for immod'rate Gain,
Too tame and paſſive to complain.

Now all the ſpeechleſs Merriment,
That Jovial Demons could invent,
Paſs'd round the Diabolick Crew,
As Mirth, which Drunkards us'd to do,
Some capering from ſide to ſide,
With Kimbo'd Arms, to ſhew their Pride,
Whilſt others rowl'd their Saucer-Eyes
About, to give the Croud ſurpriſe:
Among the reſt, who thus attend
The Doctor to his diſmal End,
A ſtrange infernal ill-look'd Fellow,
Hump-back'd and dreſs'd like Punchionello,
Appear'd ſo very Briſk and Airy,
So Active and profuſely Merry,
As if he was of high degree,
Some ruling Dev'l of Quality,

I 2   For

For in Proud *Pluto*'s wealthy Court,

Are gainful Posts of e'ery Sort,

Which makes so many Thousands here,

So vile and wicked as they are,

In hopes of great Preferments there.

    At length the fatal Hour is struck,

By some adjacent doleful Clock,

Which sound informs the Doctor's Ear,

That his sad End was drawing near,

And told him he had sin'd beyond

Relief, in signing Satan's Bond.

The Doctor, starting, looks aghast,

To hear the Clock proclaim his last,

A dismal Passing-Bell indeed,

When no Repentance can succeed;

He having left no spark of Hope,

In *Pater-Noster*, Priest, or Pope,

But from the last tremendous Hour,

Was solely in the Devil's Power,

Who now with awful Looks and Signs,

Commands his dancing Underlings,

To

To feife with fpeed the reptile Sinner

And give him *Draco* for his Dinner.

Accordingly, a Sumpter Devil,

Crook-back'd like *Æfop*, was fo civil

To mount the Doctor's driping Rump,

Upon his huge diftorted Hump;

And thus, by th' help of two Supporters,

Conveys him to his laft new Quarters,

The Dragon roaring, opens wide

His Sparrow-Mouth, from fide to fide,

And down he gulps him at one fwallow,

As glib as if he'ad all been Tallow;

Then bellow'd like a greedy Beaft,

In pain for fuch another Feaft ;

Now peals of Thunder rowl aloud,

To terrify the gazing Croud,

And render the tremendous Scene,

More frightful than it need have been ;

The Dragon roaring mounts up higher,

And gapes, to fhow his Mouth's on fire,

Which like a flaming Oven looks

When heating at the Paftry-Cooks.

Th

The Devils, to conclude the Jeſt,

Cling cloſe to the departing Beaſt,

Among the reſt the Doctor's Zany,

Who made the Croud more ſport than any,

Catch'd hold o'th' Dragons Duggs and there

He held and hung 'twixt Earth and Air,

Reſolving boldly to perſue

His Maſter's Steps, and like a true.

Kind Friend, to give the Dev'l his due:

And thus, like Witches in a Seive,

They mount the Skies and take their leave.

The Scholars, or ſome other Youngſters,

Singing the while, like doleful Songſters;

By which we do ſuppoſe they mean

To hide the ſcreeks of the Machine,

That as aloft the Dragon flies,

Our Ears ſha'n't undeceive our Eyes.

So, when an injur'd Peer is brou[...]

To die for ſome new Part[...]

Leſt Truth the Peoples Ears ſhould reach,

With Noiſe they drown his dying Speech.

F I N I S.